T0368039

Poems for Jo

DAISY CWIKLINSKI

BALBOA.PRESS
A DIVISION OF HAY HOUSE

Balboa Press books may be ordered through booksellers or by contacting:

Balboa Press
A Division of Hay House
1663 Liberty Drive
Bloomington, IN 47403
www.balboapress.com
844-682-1282

Because of the dynamic nature of the Internet, any web addresses or links contained in this book may have changed since publication and may no longer be valid. The views expressed in this work are solely those of the author and do not necessarily reflect the views of the publisher, and the publisher hereby disclaims any responsibility for them.

The author of this book does not dispense medical advice or prescribe the use of any technique as a form of treatment for physical, emotional, or medical problems without the advice of a physician, either directly or indirectly. The intent of the author is only to offer information of a general nature to help you in your quest for emotional and spiritual well-being. In the event you use any of the information in this book for yourself, which is your constitutional right, the author and the publisher assume no responsibility for your actions.

Interior Image Credit: Floyd Scott

ISBN: 979-8-7652-5793-7 (sc)
ISBN: 979-8-7652-5794-4 (e)

Library of Congress Control Number: 2024925454

Print information available on the last page.

Balboa Press rev. date: 01/23/2025

Contents

. . . .

A letter to Jo Elaine

I wish I could be writing this book on one of those suitcase typewriters we used when you took me to work. I remember the shag carpet, 60's chairs and wood paneling like I am there now.

I wish I had a particular story that was written on that machine. It was a retelling of Little Red Riding Hood, with the wolf at the helm. I guess even back then I could see the humanity in the beast.

At this very moment, my four year old son is sitting on the floor reciting scenes from the Three Little Pigs. He is *obsessed* with werewolves and storytelling.

I couldn't be more proud of him.

But none of this would be if not for you,

Love Always,
Your Daisy,
Daisy.

Not So - Fairy Tales

Brothers Grimm

There are three sides
To this Story:

The Princess
The Eldest Prince
The Little Prince

None of the narrators have been very reliable.
This is no fairytale ending.
It wasn't one to begin with

Princess:
When I was young,
I believed
There was someone for everyone.
I thought
I would find the "one,"
Then I'd be done.

In my teens
I came to the realization
That maybe there wasn't just one,
But a collection.
Sometimes, you have to kiss a frog.
Or two.
Unluckily, I somehow became thrust
Between the choices
Of two peculiar and striking princes
Desperate to be king of the castle.

I was the girl next door,
The key to the edifice's hole.

Eldest Prince:
Firstborn with a thorny crown,
Crooked smile,
Fool in ripped black skinny jeans
Spoiled rock star,
Drank away his sorrows-
Belonged to everyone and no one.

Thinking he could win the heart of the princess
By ferociously strumming his guitar
And skating around her in circles,
Cigarette smoke puffing.
Charmingly practiced
Deceivingly calculated.

The Little Prince:
Young-Blooded and Handsome
Cheerful grin,
in the perfect place at all times.

This frog was sweet and authentic.
He kissed the ground
The princess walked on.

He made attempts at winning her heart
With his boyish emotions and love of books.
He looked at her with adoration.

This Little Prince had a constant fervor
In the form of butterflies fluttering around everywhere.

The butterflies landed on the princess' shoulder
One at a time,
And then collectively
As the joy filled her entirely.

Princess:
The Little Prince clearly started as the best possible candidate.
How could the princess pass up on such pure romance?
They had a real connection.

The princess was going to kiss the frog
To bring the king out of the little prince's skin...

Until one day,
The thorny crowned prince started dancing
About her more frequently.
He was danger in sheep's clothing.

Deep down, every princess enjoys a little mystery.
A little inconsistency.

In truth,
The princess was a rather independent woman
And she wanted to be seen as such.

Not that the little prince didn't grant that wish,
But she was starting to feel that it went unrecognized.

The selfish first-born saw her for what she was
And used it against her.
It won her over.
She kissed the frog-

A catalyst to the new king's throne.

But instead of turning into the king she had previously envisioned,
The prince started to grow large oozing warts
And continued to hop around at her feet.

He always needed more,
But the more kisses she gave,
the uglier he became

Until he croaked.

The Little Prince couldn't stand to look at her.
He left her to drop to the ground,
Head in hands, sobbing.

She chose wrong.

She was only left with herself.
To take the blame.

Peter Pan and the Lost Girl

You were Peter Pan
and I
Your Lost Girl.

Not quite Wendy,
But just as wild and free.

That fiery red hair of yours,
Never growing up-
It drew me in.

You were like a safe haven—
Always wanting to take care of me,
Providing a place to rest my swarmed head.

The dream to move away from the white noise
Was just that,
A dream.

The king of the Lost Boys,
Can only be a ruler in Neverland.
You weren't fit to live in the confines of suits and ties.

I belong to the wild unknown.
You might find me awake in the middle of the night-
Following the moon down some dark alleyway.
I have remained lost forever.
I don't know that I will ever be found.

We are too similar,
You and I.

The Perks of Dating a Wallflower

Sometimes,
I think about lying with you on carpeted floors,
Just to be closer to one another.

I think about the first time
You held my hand,
Under that furry black blanket.

I think about how awkward
Our first kiss was,
But also how authentic.

Can we have a re-do?

I think about the time we stayed awake
Until past dawn,
Talking about nothing and everything in between.

I think about when you visited me at work,
Twice in one night.
How mad it made everyone,
How happy it made me.

I think about that night you came over,
When I needed to run away.

My life was a mess of cardboard boxes
and peace-seeking monsters.

All I needed was you,

The mossy golf course forest
And the twinkling lights above,

That night will forever be covered in shiny plastic wrap.
Preserved from the aftermath.

Everything was perfect
Until the fear of moving sank in

Avoidance of what we were both really feeling.

I blamed the crumbling remains,
Broken twigs
and stardust on you,

But really, it was my fault.
I should've told you that I was falling
Like beams in the sky.

Instead of remembering all of the wonder-filled times
We created,

I remained in my state
Of hating you
for breaking
What wasn't ever ours

You gave me a sense of nostalgia
That has now become
A shot in the dark.

Casper the Broken Ghost

The way you loved me
Mimicked
Falling leaves

Red
Orange
Yellow
Brown

I am no fortune teller,
But I should have seen the heartbreak coming,
A mile away.

I knew the moment you bore your ochre eyes
into mine,
My whole world would come crashing down
In ruins and piles of dust.

I knew it from the start,
But, I still entered
That deep, dark cave

Wide-eyed,
Arms stretched as wide
As the northern hemisphere

I knew you were a masterpiece
Hidden behind
Broken glass
And shredded metal.

I didn't care.

All I ever wanted,
Was to hold you close,
So that my beating heart
Would glue yours
Back together.

I would chase you around
Every wooded wonderland.
Every dusty maze of books piled high.

We were a story
Waiting to be told.

Waterfalls and neighborhood parks
Obscure coffee shops with rose flavored drips
Vintage records from *Magnolia Thunder Pussy*
Pink Rabbits and melted sandwiches
Long walks
Night talks

Life stories inked on our skin
Held in our bones.
Memories of two souls
Sound-tracked.

I used to see forever,
Under your gaze.

If only we could've really been
Runaways.
I'd go to Heaven and Hell,
Sit in Purgatory,
Just to be by your side.

I'll love you till my heart stops beating
And blood drains from every limb,
There's no denying that.

The Girl Who Cried Wolf

I should've known
When I met you,
My life would be
Turned upside down.

You changed me,
in the worst way-
Took what wasn't yours,
And ran.

I should have known the signs.
I should have listened to the white noise.
I should have looked more closely
At those perfectly sharpened teeth
And hateful eyes filled with venom.

I should have been able to look into that gaze,
and follow it down to the
Depths of hell
That is your soul.

I should've known Little Red
Doesn't get through the forest
Unharmed.

I should have known that you were the hunter
Come to collect.

But I didn't know.
I was blind,
Naïve.
I let fear shock me still.

So still, that all I could do,
Was lie back and
Watch.

I should have cried wolf.
I didn't have the courage
To muster anything above a whisper
So silent
I couldn't even hear it.

I was weak under your hold.

I stood back,

Watched as you devoured me alive
Slowly and painfully.

All I wanted to do was make it
To grandma's house
Before dark.

I didn't make it.

Little Red isn't so little anymore.

When you spit me back up,
I'd grown-
Like Jack's beanstalk.

I grew tired.

Where that
Fresh
Flushed
Flesh
Used to sit porcelain still,
Is now cracked and battered.

The light in my eyes is gone,
Replaced by a fire that is built to burn
You to ashes.

That frail skeletal system
That once stood
Is now
Muscle and bone.

You see,
In that short time,
In your abdomen,
I grew strong.
I grew spite.
I grew anger.
I grew hate.

So thank you
For chewing away
At my innocence,

For now,
I am wiser than before.

What Goes On
Behind Closed Doors

Chain-Link Fence

I'm bound inside
This
Chain
Link
Fence

The Wall of Constriction
Tempts me,
To make my
Escape.

If only I were a little taller,

I could reach
High Above
And
Overcome
This
Great Obstacle

If only I were a little taller

My Body
Fills
With
Regret

For what I have done.

Now,
I'm Bound
To this
Chain
Link
Fence

I Can't Go There

I can't go up on the hill
To look at the stars.

I can't go to my local Starbucks
To drink gingerbread lattes.

I can't go to the Marsh Creek caves
To ponder the world.

I can't go to the Solano drive-in
To watch movies outside.

Without thinking of you.

I still wonder if you are okay.
I still think of you every day.
I still want to know how you're doing.
I still worry about the sharks while you're surfing.
I still have concerns when it comes to the drugs.
I still hope the court isn't beating you up.
I still care.

I keep telling myself

I'm happier
I'm better off without you
I have someone better
I don't need you

But somehow the ghost of you remains in the back of my mind at all times.

Come As You Are

I've traveled
Far and Wide
Through
Many
Different Times,

I've seen
Fire
&
I've seen
Rain

I've seen
Sunny Days,
I thought would
Never end.

At night,
I wake up with
The sheets
Soaking wet.
A freight train
Running through
The middle of
My head.

Only you can
Cool my
Desire.

So,
You think you
Could tell

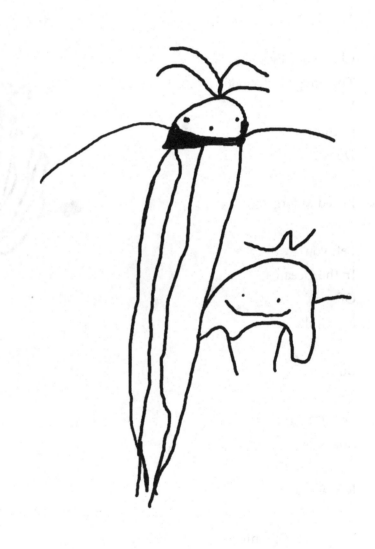

Heaven
From
Hell?

Burning every bridge
You cross,
Looking for
Some beautiful place
To get lost?

Close your Eyes.
That long black cloud
Is
Coming
Down.

I tried to forget,

Left you
In the Ocean
Of
My Guilt.

But,

You grew
Roots
Around my
Ribcage

You have done things
You cannot *imagine*
You would
Ever
Do.

Free as a Bird,
Born to Run.

You will
Suffer.

You will
Want to
Die.

Sing me to sleep,
I'm tired
And I
Want to go to
Bed.

Tell Everyone I'm Leaving,
But I Won't Be Gone For Long

"The Mind
Becomes a place,
The Soul
Goes to hide,
From The Heart."

I tried to erase you
From my memory,

So that you wouldn't
Leave Imprints
On my Skin.

I wasted all of my best
Material
On You.

And now,
It's quite literally
Gone With the Wind.

Bodies

Bodies
Bodies
Everywhere

Let's Talk About Sex

Put On a Show

Putting on a show
Is my specialty,

Lately,
It has me thinking:
It's my destiny.

Maybe that's what happens,
When your Virginity
Is Stolen.

Leaves your heart feeling swollen,

Until it bursts,
With all of the distrust for everyone,

Especially your dad,
Because maybe if he was around more,

But instead, we're always moving.
And he's still always gone.

And I still feel most at home
On the road.

Funny how
the things that
Tear us apart,
Somehow
Bring us back,
Together.

It doesn't mend your soul,
But provides understanding.

You see,
From the outside.

Ask why I'm not
Like that at
Home.

I tell you,
Home is *different*.
Where you shouldn't
Have to Hide.

Maybe,
That's why this House
has *never*
Felt like
Home.

Because,
You can't Heal
where you got Sick.

And I don't even want to try.

Too many times you've seen me cry,
To not wipe away the tears.

I can't wait an indeterminate amount of years
For you to See

All I ever wanted,
Was a House
that felt like
Home.

I don't want to keep wearing a mask,
Putting on a Show,

Living in a
Circus.

Because,
You could *never*
See Me
Unconditionally.

Could *never* care for me,
The way I
Needed.

I won't continue
To let myself
Bleed.

Good at Faking It

Sex to me,
Is by all accounts,
Transactional.

Walk into my
Office,
Like it's
Business.

Tell me
You want to
Fuck Me,
Because we only have
10 Minutes.

You say it feels
Emotionless.

Don't care
That it's an
Act,
For Me.

I will
get you off,
Bringing you to
Your knees.

Making Pleas.

Begging Please.

It's a
Sick
Sadistic
Game
We Play.

You want
To have
Control.

But,
This has to be
On my
Terms.

Less work,
For you.

Setting your
Inferiority Complex
On fire.

I never tried
Faking it,
For the record.

It was you,
I wanted
To please.

I knew,
You would never
Make me
Finish.

But,
Didn't want you
To get
Discouraged.

But,
Then,
You got Cocky,

And I couldn't
Just let you
Have it.

Couldn't lie,
To make You
Feel better.

That's how I knew,
I was good
At faking it.

Tell Me I'm Pretty

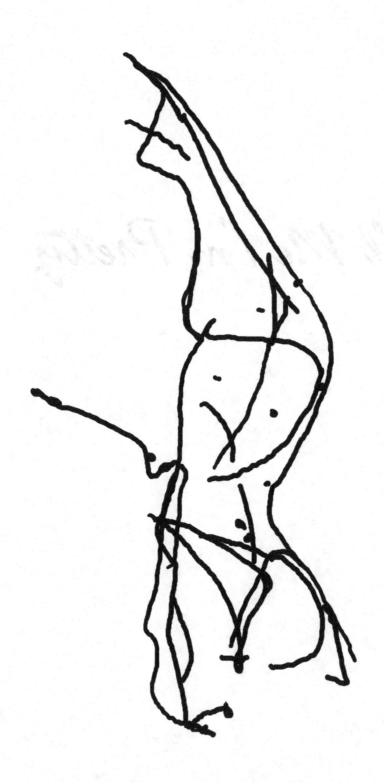

We All Live in the Dollhouse

We all Live,
In the
Dollhouse.

With each our Roles,
To play.

We never go Outside.
Because,
Everyday,
Is a
Rainy Day.

Inside
&
Out.

On the
Highest Shelf,
Out of
Reach,

To keep the
Monsters
At Bay.

Luckily,
They don't
Make the Effort,
To Climb.

I grew up here,
I'll die here.

Agoraphobic
By nature.

Never seeing,
Sunlight.

Trapped,
Behind walls.
Never going,
From
Room,

To
Room.

Never,
In the
Basement.

They say,
Acceptance,
Is the Gift,
You give,
Yourself.

But,
I haven't
Been in a
Giving Mood.

Not to *Myself,*
Not to **Anyone.**

I don't even know,
What it is like,
To want,
To leave,

I have no
Concept,
Of where,
I'd be
Leaving,
To.

The Pedestal

All I ever wanted
Was for you to play with me

Instead, you kept me
On a shelf

Your perfect doll

You need the smile plastered on my face

You need me on this ledge

Your little girl that won't make a sound
Won't move an inch

I'll sit here and be your punching bag
You control when I come down.
You control what I endure

Because I'm spineless
Can't move under your hold
I just want it to end

So, I seek out others.
Who put me on their shelves
And wait for them to play with me

But I only get taken down
For narcissistic pleasure

You molded me
When I just wanted you
To take me down.

And play with me
I'm getting really tired of being
Up on this shelf

Smile painted on my face

You've turned everyone
Who looks at me
Into a *collector*

For a while it was nice
I must be pretty
Special
For all to want me
Up on their shelves

They stare at me
Throughout the day

I hardly ever get picked up
And when I do,

It's never for very long

Just enough
To get some *Satisfaction*

So there I sit

And then they realize
I am out of fashion
Broken
Or
Unhinged

In some way
Damaged Goods

So they go out
And find a new model

With longer hair
A different shade of peach

Maybe this time
She will be
Russet

Her eyes will twinkle

But you keep me
On your shelf

No matter
How Ragged my
Edges are

You need me this way

Mostly Destroyed

But that smile...

It's painted on
So it *never* fades

You need me to sit still
And look pretty

Up on this
shelf

I can't speak
I can't close
My eyes

Not that I'd be able to
Otherwise

Other dolls come and go

But not a single one
Can replace
The *hours*
Of work

You've put
Into molding me

My Ears are clogged
My Eyes in a stagnant position
These big
Smiling Lips
They are glued shut

You do this so no
Evil
Escapes

So here I sit
Waiting for some other
Domino
To push me
Off this ledge

Maybe then
My face
Would *shatter*

I sit here waiting
For the moment
Gravity takes its toll

And cracks this smile.

Completely Mental &
Certifiably Insane

Dysmorphia For Animals

Sometimes I feel
Like a
Fatted Calf
Off to
The
Slaughter

Ironic

She is Slipping
Through
The
Cracks

As the
Disorder
Attacks

Deep
in her
Veins

Poisonous Black Venom
Swallows her
Whole
Engulfing her Soul

Until all that's left is

Skin
&
Bone.

Joints
Melted
Away

Translucency

Looking

In the

Oval Glass
Seeing
Warped
Visions

Where
Her Skeleton
Resides.

A microscopic Vision

With
a
Solid
Steel
Mallet,

She Smashes into
a
Million Shards.

All *unique*
In
SIZE
&
SHAPE

Mania

First
       I see the red car
              It zooms by and starts to look like **FIRE**
Now
       I see
              A line of **RED** cars

Some on the Right side. Some on the Left.
THEN
       I hear the *wind*
              It Blows the Trees
                  & the Leaves
                    & the Grass
                        UNTIL
                    It reaches the *Flowers*.

NOW
       I hear construction
              The Powerful Machines
                  Are Heard from Miles away
       I hear a car **BEEP**
              A Man's **YELL**

The same red car passes.
       Slower this time
Now, a silver car passes
       Directing my eyes to the sky
              It's blue with puffy things
              Called clouds

I smell the fresh air
       Filled with Hot Humidity

Nothing Happens

Until

ALL OF A SUDDEN

A Loud Bang
      Drawing my ears to the Mower
Now, a white car passes
      Before my very eyes
          Now, I am paying Attention

To **COLORS**
  Green
      Green is **EVERYWHERE**
  Yellow
      I spot the Hydrant
         Then the Butterfly
         Then a Bird
            Then Another Butterfly

But this one is white.
      And chasing a blackbird!

All the while
      2 Planes Go By Ahead
More Cars pass.
      BEEP
         SLAM
            ZOOM

More wind blows
      The Birds Chirp
         A cricket Hums

And a Black car.
    That goes back and Forth
        Up & Down
             The street
Then the white butterfly
      Comes back into View

I'm Too Drunk to Drive

And that scares
The shit
Out of
Me

What if my
Son
Needs a
Colostomy?

Would my
Grandmother
Be Ashamed
Of Me?

Would she
Understand?

I miss her
So
Goddamn
Much.

I wish
She was
Here.

I'm going
Through
So
Much
Shit
Right
Now.

BUT

I think

She can be
Everywhere
At once.

I can talk
To her
Daily

But it just
Isn't the
Same
&
It NEVER
Will be.

Baby Bird

Little Birds
Dancing in my Head
Leaving multicolored sheaths
of skin behind,
as I walk through The Valley of Death.
****
I still look at myself in the mirror,
Wondering:
who is this stranger reflected back
through plated glass?

We could be *twins*.

The half that has her life together,

The *other half*,
Unsure
Insecure
jagged,
a missing piece.

We share
Memories
Feelings
Hopes
Dreams

But we are different beings entirely.
Split personalities
Shaped by conceptual realities.

One is the angel
Out to slay the misfortunes of humanity,

The other,
a dark demon soul
Feeding off the pain of the Damned.
An Internal Compass points North
Of whomever outstretches their *veins*
close enough.

Sending them out
into the massive crashing waves,
To become limping shipwrecks

Until eyes run black,
And all of humanity sinks down
Like witches tied to rocks.

The girl in the reflected light is in despair.
She sees me standing there,
Above the wreckage
She only wanted to create Eden
Out of the Wasteland.

It isn't long until the glass is shattered
And out from the ashes rises a phoenix.

The Monsters Inside Us

Close my eyes
And strip away the
White *noise*
Around me.

I never hear
The word escape,
Without a quicker
Blood.

No word is strong—
Yet *gentile*
Enough.

Is it waterproof?
Shatterproof?
Proof against fire?
And bombs
Through the roof?

Fears stood tall,
Like giants.

Mountains toppling evermore
Into seas
Without a Shore

They use the moon no more
For the same end as before.

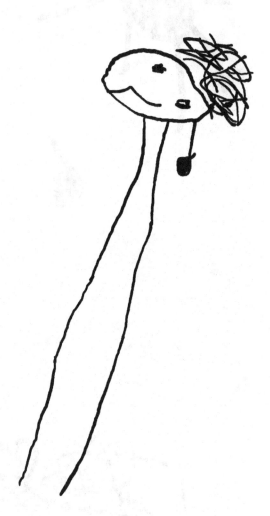

Miss Carried

Little Universe

Being pregnant is like having a little universe inside of you.
One that grows and grows.
But sometimes, it dies.
Sometimes, it happens at the same time.

It should be easier the less time it takes up space, right?
It should be easier once you have released one previously, right?
That hasn't made it any easier.

There wasn't any preparation.
It doesn't matter that the beginning had a low percentage of continuing.
Nothing makes it easier.

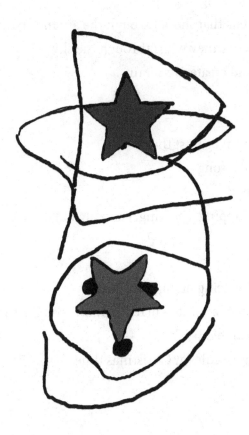

A Blessing in Disguise

A heartbeat
A breath
A cry
A laugh

These are the sounds
You will
Never
Hear.

I will *never* see
My own reflection
The orange-red that fades to purple sun-set and rise
Butterflies resting on a bright yellow tulip
The neon flicker of a lightning bug
Reds and blues and greens that shoot through the air and sparkle and fizzle out
Red-brown falling leaves as they whirl through the sky
Flakes that fall gently and create mountains.

I will *never* hear
The soothing drum of rain against the roof
The unique heartbeat of a song
The hum of guitar strings
The sound of a crowd clapping, cheering, carrying out a beat.

I will *never* smell
The thick smoke of a fire being lit on a chilly night
The sugary combination of a roasted marshmallow atop melting chocolate
Nor the musty smell of an old book
Not even the minty pine needles at Christmas time.

I will *never* taste
The flavors of baby food
Frozen ice cream on the roof of my mouth
Melting cotton candy the moment it touches my tongue
Clean, refreshing breeze.

I will *never* feel
A doll's silky hair
An affectionate, warm kiss goodnight
Arms wrapped tightly around me
Tears running down my face, becoming warm as they dry
An everlasting love
A crushing heartbreak
A symbol of infinity on my left hand.

I will *never* experience
Tiptoeing down the long, dark hall in the middle of the night
My hair swirling in the wind like a tornado when all of the windows are rolled down
The last dance, carefully measured, forcing a sway
Vows being read by a lifelong friend
Holding an angel of my own
The sad sorrow of everyone dressed in black.

I was only two trimesters away.

You Have Been Healed

Floyd's Travel Guide

The lonesome magnolia
Wanders
Wistfully

Is it
Serendipity?

The Wild Universe
Is a
Cocoon
Of
Flora
&
Fauna?

Lost
in the
Scrumptious
Euphoria
Of
Nostalgia,
Luna & Stella
Converge
Disjointed
In
Guise

The Indie-Hippie & Bohemian
Embark
On a Journey
Through
Dystopian
Gravel

Mountains
&
Limestone
Trails

Creating
Alien Amethyst Crystals
While
Meditating
On
Jupiter
Such
Harrowing
Pompous
Anamorphic
Pluviophiles!

What
Electric Cacophony!

It takes Courage
To
Wander
Through
Ocean
Waves

The Greatest Adventure
Through
Psychedelic
Disillusionment.

Home

Home:
Has *never* been a
House

It is the
Wide Open Road—

That Collection of Places
I have seen along that Expanse.

I have always considered
The Ocean, The Mountains & The Forest
A greater source of Shelter than

Stucco
Brick
Siding
Molds

These are mere cases
To store your Belongings
Until
The next Adventure
Rolls Around

These Molds,
So Temporary
Can be Infringed Upon
At any given
Moment.

Existence
Was meant for more than
Four Walls

There is a
Hunger
For something
Greater

That pushes
Boundaries

Goes against
Popularity

& measurable
Sanity.

There is a
Whole World
Out There

Most only See through
Paper Maps & Mechanical Telescopes

One Cannot Experience
The Abundance Of Life
In this
Sheltered Aversion

Forever My Anchor

You'd think I know a lot about
Cancer
With the amount of times
I've witnessed
It.

I hope I never have to deal with it
First Hand

Deal with It
Is an interesting turn of phrase
Isn't it?

But

Here I am
Listening to an audiobook
After dropping my son off at
School

& it's talking about
Death
&
Hospice
&
Cancer

That was caught too
Late
To do anything
About

This is not the book
I signed up for.

I signed up for
BODIES IN THE BASEMENT,

But this is why I am writing this
Now.

How could I not include
Cancer
In a *story*
About my life.
When it has been so *o m n i p r e s e n t*

When it took away my
Anchor.

Speaking of it
REALLY
Annoys me when people comment
On
Anchor
Tattoos

"I refuse to sink"
"All anchors do are sink"

You dumbasses,

They hold the goddamn
Boat
Afloat.

SO THE BOAT DOESN'T SINK

It's degrading

We are
Ships
With Rooms
We are
Large
Vessels
&
We are
Shaky
Without our
Anchors

Why do you think
So

Many

People

talk about

Drowning?

Stay Afloat
&
Know the
Anchors
Will
Protect
You

I have a
Different
Type of
Anchor
Tattoo

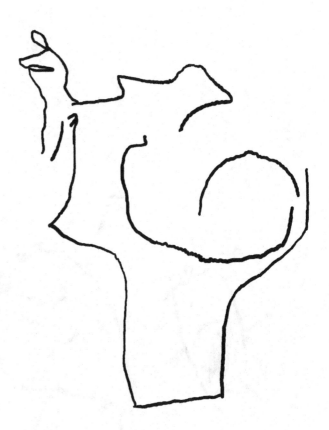

Poems For Michael

Washing Dishes

I like to imagine you
Bending me over,
While I'm
Washing Dishes,

Scrubbing Away the
Screaming Demons
Inside my Head

Sudsing every
Bad Memory,

Making my Brain
Squeaky Clean.

Abandoned Buildings

You
Set
All of *My*
Abandoned Buildings
On Fire

&

From the
Ashes
I
Build
Anew

Never Sleep Again

I'm gonna make you SCREAM
Beyond your wildest dreams
With these tales from the Crypt
And I ain't even got a script

Gotta take cover
'Cause I know what you did
Last Summer.

It's the end of the book
If you get caught
By the hook.

Get under the bed fast,
So you end up with the knife
In your back last.

It's the night of the Purge,
And I'm afraid to emerge

Sew Eyes on my Hands
And call me the Pale Man

Might turn you into a lampshade
If Dahmer goes on a crusade.

They're coming at me with scissors
Screaming GET OUT!

Might just go down to the sunken place
To lose my face
to my reflection,
Searching for a real connection.

Call on the witch
'Cause the doctor is ill
And Hyde gives me the
Chills.

Saw Freddy in my nightmare
He was ripping off my clothes
Trying to step inside my soul
But he's got knives instead of fingers

I need to be exorcized
To fight these demons inside

I need the nun to come and save me tonight
But when I lifted up her hood
She gave me such a fright

Saw Michael in the field and Jason in the lake
You won't know your fate
Because Michael is the Boogieman
And Jason is a hockey fan

Chucky and his wife always end in a fight
But, don't turn out the lights
Because Jigsaw and Annabelle just might get
Married tonight

We'll all float down here
If Pennywise
Gets between her thighs.

Dead silence when Carrie comes in
Because she ain't afraid of no Pig.

Say their names three times in the mirror,
And they are sure to appear

Open elevators with blood
The night might end in a flood.

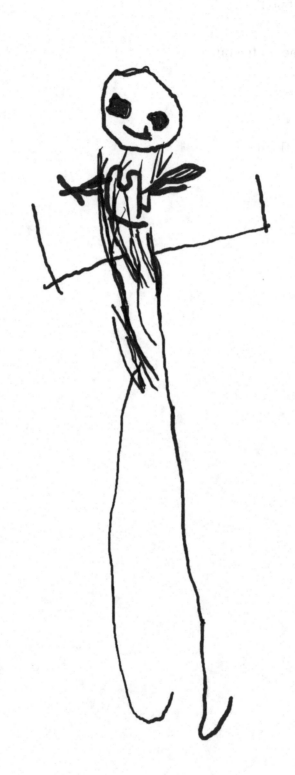

About The Author

....

Daisy is an upcoming poet and novelist, with a background in Design and Psychology.

Since early childhood, she has always had her nose in a book and fingers on a word processor. She has won first place in a writing competition for scriptwriting, and honorable mention for *The Girl Who Cried Wolf*.

She now resides with her family in Northern California, and is working on a thriller and memoir.

Acknowledgments

Floyd Orion Alfalfa, you are the center of my universe. You will always be the first person I thank. You saved my life the moment you became a cluster of cells inside of me. I would not be here today if you did not come along. You are, and always will be my greatest gift and my strongest inspiration to keep going.

Light of my life, fire of my loins, I heard a Post Malone song that said, "who am I to write rock bottom from the highs you took me to?" I could not have said this sentiment any better.

You will always be my first reader, my greatest supporter. You have held up the mirror I never wanted, but always needed.

From the very beginning, I knew we had been lovers in a past life – that we will always find each other in every future life.

I am having the most intense writer's block after this book, because you have provided such a safe and healing environment. I am depleting the well more and more every day, in the best possible way.

Tiaunta, you are the sister I never had and the best aunt I could have ever dreamed of for Floyd. Even when he learns to fully pronounce your name, you will forever be his Tiaunta.

You have kept it real with me from the very beginning and that means the world to me. I can always rely on you for the hard truth and consistency. You've been around since Floyd's inception, through every big moment. Thank you for being such an integral part of our lives.

Bubba, my spooky Thing Two, you entered my life at one of the most pivotal moments. I know you would go to Hell and back with me with a suitcase full of souvenirs, to remind us of the journey for years to come.

You are fiercely loyal, and I can't wait to haunt everyone in the afterlife together. You think of all sides and the emotions that go into it. You remind me of who I am to my core when I fall and lose my way. You have shown me that it is ok to not be ok – to truly believe it; to pick myself up and dust myself off.

And to the readers for going down this journey with me, one word at a time.

A final special acknowledgment to all the writers who have come before me. I have been so inspired by your works, that I have knitted some of my favorite lines into my found poems.

I Will Tell About It: Sharon Olds, "I Go Back to May 1937" & Anna Peters, "I Tried to Forget"

The Monsters Inside Us: Emily Dickenson, "I never hear the word "Escape" (144)", Sylvia Plath, "The Applicant" & Edgar Allen Poe, "Nevermore"

Take Me As I Come: Pink Floyd, "Wish You Were Here", Joy Division, "Wilderness", Bruce Springsteen, "Born to Run" & "I'm On Fire", Lynyrd Skynyrd, "Free Bird", Bob Dylan, "Knockin' on Heaven's Door", James Taylor, "Fire and Rain", The Smiths, "Asleep" & Elliot Smith, "Let's Get Lost"

Printed in the United States
by Baker & Taylor Publisher Services